What MAGIC Can I Create Today?

Book Cover, Typesetting and Layout Design Copyright © 2023 Maja Creative
Art Direction by Maja Wolnik of Maja Creative
Graphic Design by Monika Brzeczek of Maja Creative
ISBN PRINT 978-0-6457403-0-1
ISBN EBOOK 978-0-6457403-1-8

What MAGIC Can I Create Today?

POSITIVE AFFIRMATIONS
BY SARAH ARTHUR-YOUNG

This book is dedicated to you, the most amazing individual that has ever walked this planet.

May everything in your universe be filled with success, love and happiness.

Wishing all loved ones, friends and families to be filled with abundance and prosperity.

May this book make an impact in your life now and forever.

Love Sarah xx

I´m happy, healthy,
VIBRANT AND WISE
full of energy and strength
TO ACHIEVE whatever I wish
TO ACHIEVE

be
THE ENERGY
you want
TO ATTRACT

Whether you are at school, hanging out with your friends, or at home with your family, siblings and parents - always have and be the energy you want around you.

It might be hard sometimes to put a smile on your face.

When you are positive and happy you will receive so much more happiness and positivity, everyone will love to be around you, and you will feel amazing.

You must love you!

You are so important in this world and have so much to give. You are unique. You really can achieve anything you want to, you just need to put your mind to it and do what makes your heart sing.

What makes you happy? What makes you smile? What makes you laugh?

Do more of that!

I LOVE and approve OF MYSELF

May I RECEIVE WHAT I'VE been praying FOR

Happiness is a choice.

No one will ever make you happy until you choose to be happy.

Smile, smile, smile.

Laugh, laugh, laugh.

We sometimes get stuck doing the same thing all the time and we are left wondering why we get the same result and things don't work out the way we want them to.

So, if you choose a different path, you will get a different outcome.

YOU ARE limitless. WHAT ARE YOU waiting for?

What are you REFUSING to let go of?

If you only choose to let go,
life would be so easy?

Don't let anyone tell you that you aren't beautiful or handsome. Don't change who you are for anyone.

People will always love you for who you are!

You are special. You are a unique individual.

Be Real

BE RAW,

Be You!

I am OPEN TO manifesting ABUNDANCE today

We all have the power to create the outcome whether it be good or bad.

Sometimes we get so caught up in an outcome that we forget to just go with the flow and let life unfold.

What's done is done.
Just breathe... you are amazing.

WE DON'T *grow* if *we live* IN THE PAST. WE NEED TO *let go, and* MOVE ON.

You will ALWAYS RECEIVE abundance AND MORE from THE universe IF YOU GIVE OUT love AND POSITIVITY

Today's a good day because
I'm going to make it a good day.

Spend more time with people who are good
for your mental health.

People who make you happy.

People who are good for your soul.

People who make your heart sing.

LEAVE
footprints
OF LOVE and
KINDNESS
everywhere
YOU GO

I love it when UNEXPECTED things happen

Always say thank you and be grateful for
every day you are healthy, happy, and alive.

I am grateful for my healthy body.
I am grateful for my loving parents.
I am grateful for my life.
I am grateful for my friends.
I am grateful for my brothers and sisters.

I love my life.

What energy space and consciousness can my body and I be today to live in the highest potential of love and happiness?

Perfect
DIVINE
Timing.
EVERYTHING WILL FALL INTO PLACE...
be patient

FOLLOW YOUR heart, it knows THE WAY and will never LEAD YOU ASTRAY

Love whole heartedly.
Give and you shall receive.

Choose to give love every time.

Sometimes this can be hard to do when people don't respect you, but the easiest thing to do is walk away from an argument.

Hold your head up high and forgive them for their wrong doing.

I AM VIBRATING
love out
OF MY *body*
AND LOVE IS
vibrating
BACK TO ME

I am
BLESSED

Dear Universe,

I am open to allowing abundance and prosperity to flow into my life.

I am open to creating the highest, grandest vision possible of myself and my life.

You become what you believe in.

What you gain in life is far greater than what you give up.

We need to learn to be kind to one another.

If you treat people badly and do the wrong thing by that person, life will always give you what you deserve.

We are all energy and connected. Give out into the universe what you wish to receive in return.

I am
GRATEFUL
for the
LITTLE THINGS

be clear
OF WHAT YOU WANT
to attract
INTO YOUR LIFE

Smile at someone random today!

Love is the only way.

I express my gratitude.

I believe in me.

My thoughts become things.

Be happy and smile.

I believe.

Overthinking can create problems
that don't exist!

I am aligned with my highest vibration and
there I create peace naturally.

BE A powerful CREATOR

THANK YOU
universe
FOR ME

Thank you universe for my beautiful body.

Thank you universe for my beautiful eyes.

Thank you universe for my beautiful smile.

Thank you, universe, for the amazing
house I live in.

Thank you universe for my amazing
parents.

Thank you universe for my health.

Thank you universe for my loving nature.

Thank you, universe, for my success.

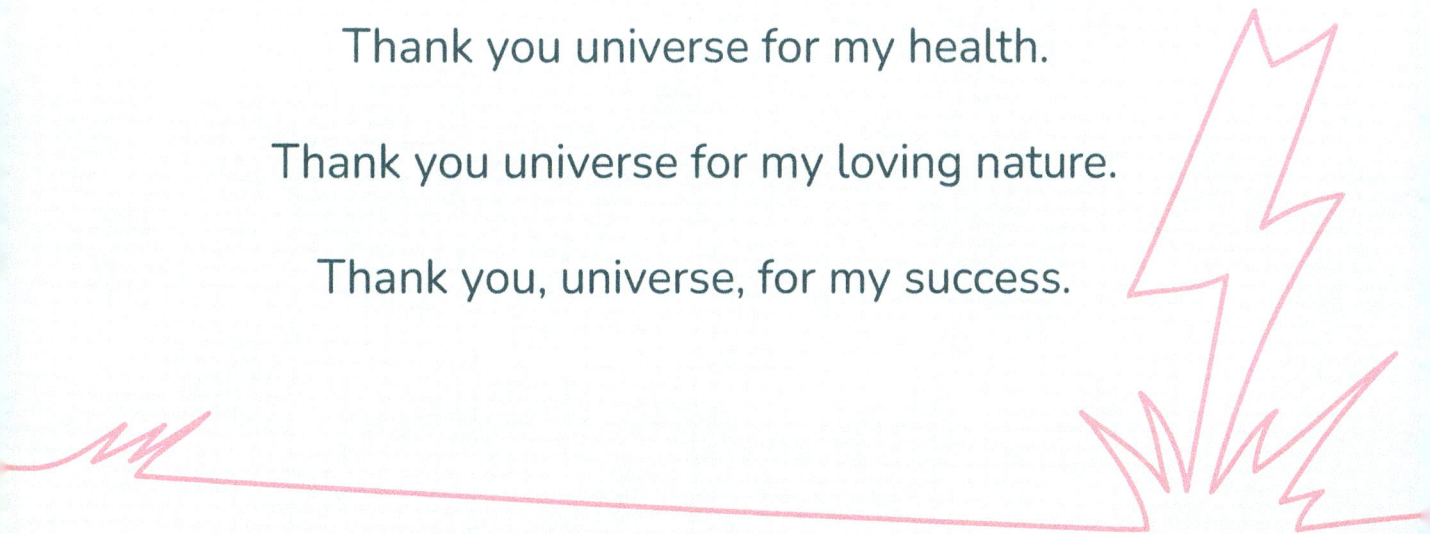

about the author
SARAH ARTHUR—YOUNG

Sarah Arthur-Young uttered her first affirmation when she was just 14 years old, when her amazing high school teacher asked her students to create their own affirmation to repeat during a meditation class.

Since then, Sarah has been using positive affirmations every day to keep on track with her goals and to align herself with the highest vibration of the universe. Affirmations have helped her cope with many of life's challenges including her parents' divorce when she herself was a child.

What Magic Can I Create Today is Sarah's first book intended to empower children and teenagers to be the best person they can possibly be.

Sarah Arthur-Young lives in Melbourne, Australia with her partner George, their son Ethan and her two stepdaughters Jordyn and Elle. When not repeating powerful affirmations, Sarah manages her finance company Say Say Money and enjoys staying healthy and active.

WWW.WHATMAGICCANICREATETODAY.COM.AU

www.ingramcontent.com/pod-product-compliance
Lightning Source LLC
Chambersburg PA
CBHW062006090426
42811CB00005B/765